DISCARD

NORMAL PUBLIC LIBRARY
206 W. COLLEGE AVE.
NORMAL, IL 61761

DEMCO

Puerto Rico

HOWARD GUTNER

Children's Press®
An Imprint of Scholastic Inc.
New York   Toronto   London   Auckland   Sydney
Mexico City   New Delhi   Hong Kong
Danbury, Connecticut

Content Consultant

Eva Cristina Vásquez
Assistant Professor of Spanish at York College
City University of New York
New York, NY

Library of Congress Cataloging-in-Publication Data

Gutner, Howard.
  Puerto Rico / by Howard Gutner.
     p. cm. — (A true book)
  Includes index.
     ISBN-13: 978-0-531-16893-6 (lib. bdg.) 978-0-531-21360-5 (pbk.)
     ISBN-10: 0-531-16893-X (lib. bdg.) 0-531-21360-9 (pbk.)

1. Puerto Rico—Juvenile literature. I. Title. II. Series.

  F1965.3.G88 2009
  972.95—dc22   2008014789

Produced by Weldon Owen Education Inc.

1 2 3 4 5 6 7 8 9 10 R 18 17 16 15 14 13 12 11 10 09

Find the Truth!

Everything you are about to read is true *except* for one of the sentences on this page.

Which one is **TRUE**?

T or F   Tiny frogs can rain from trees in Puerto Rico.

T or F   Puerto Rico consists of one island.

Find the answers in this book.

Contents

El Morro Fortress

The ceiba, or silk cotton tree, grows to an enormous size and lives for more than 300 years. ➡

THE **BIG** TRUTH!

The Big Dish

Amapola flower

Coquí frogs have become a symbol of Puerto Rico. They are named for the sound of their "ko–KWEE" call. The small frogs are light enough to glide to the ground from treetops.

CHAPTER 1

A Land of Enchantment

The first people to settle in Puerto Rico arrived about 3,000 years ago. Spanish explorers arrived later, in the late 1400s. They found **indigenous** communities, spectacular beaches, and lush forests. There were countless plants and animals they had never seen before. They called the island *La Isla del Encanto*, or "the Island of Enchantment."

It "rains" frogs in the forest when coquís jump off tall trees to escape danger.

Nature's Bounty

Puerto Rico was created by a volcano millions of years ago. The island has more than 300 miles (480 kilometers) of coastline on the Caribbean Sea. Inland are steep, tall mountains and thick, green rain forests.

Over the years, much of Puerto Rico's forest has been cut down to clear room for farms and factories and to create lumber. Many Puerto Ricans are working to protect what they still have. They have created nature reserves such as El Yunque (el YOON-kay) National Forest. Many animal species are now protected by law.

The iguanas of Mona Island, Puerto Rico, are found nowhere else in the world.

The largest animals in El Yunque include rats, bats, and brown pelicans. The animals in Puerto Rico flew or swam to the island long ago. Larger animals couldn't make the trip.

El Morro is the largest fort in the Caribbean. The Spanish began constructing it in 1539. The finished fort has tunnels, dungeons, and round sentry boxes called *garitas*.

CHAPTER 2

Tropical Isles

Puerto Rico is part of the Antilles **archipelago**, or chain of islands. These islands mark the boundary between the Caribbean Sea and the Atlantic Ocean. Other islands in this chain include Cuba, Jamaica, the Bahamas, and many other smaller islands.

The Puerto Rico parrot is one of the ten most endangered birds in the world.

Most Puerto Ricans live on a rectangular island called Puerto Rico. Several much smaller islands also belong to Puerto Rico. Three smaller islands are called Vieques, Mona, and Culebra. Vieques is the largest, although only about 10,000 people live there. Mona has no people and a large population of sea turtles, birds, and other wildlife. Culebra has fewer than 2,000 people. It is surrounded by 20 smaller **coral** islands.

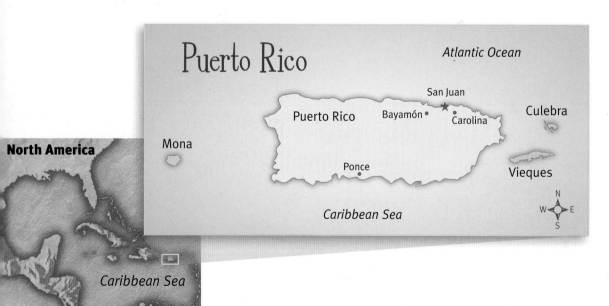

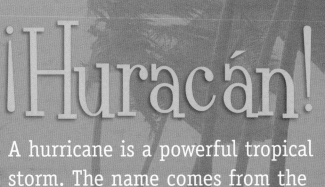

¡Huracán!

A hurricane is a powerful tropical storm. The name comes from the Taíno (tah-EE-noh) god of fierce winds—*Huracán*. The Taíno are a people who have lived in Puerto Rico for hundreds of years.

Hurricanes hit Puerto Rico about once every ten years. In the past, many homes and businesses were destroyed. Now an early warning system is in place to protect people.

Changing Jobs

Warm temperatures and consistent rainfall make about one-third of Puerto Rico's land ideal for agriculture. Long ago, small farms were replaced by large ones growing **commercial crops**. Foods such as sugarcane, bananas, pineapples, and coffee are sold outside Puerto Rico. Most are sold to the mainland United States. Puerto Ricans now eat mainly **imported** food.

Coffee plants were probably first brought to Puerto Rico by the Spanish. The climate in the central mountain ranges is perfect for growing coffee.

An increasing number of tourists are attracted by Puerto Rico's culture and natural beauty. Hotels line Isla Verde Beach in San Juan.

In the early 1900s, the economy of Puerto Rico was based on farming. In 1948, a politician named Teodoro Moscoso began to encourage U.S. businesses to build factories in Puerto Rico. For the first time, manufacturing became key to the economy. Although many of these factories closed, newer factories now produce goods such as medicines, scientific instruments, and clothing. More recently, the tourism industry has also grown. Today, manufacturing and tourism are greater sources of income than farming.

Ancient carvings by the Taíno people can be seen in the town of Utuado. The goddess Atabey is often shown with frog legs. The Taíno believed that this goddess created humankind.

CHAPTER 3

An Island in Time

An early people of Puerto Rico are called the Taíno. They traveled to the island from South America about 1,000 years ago. The Taíno were farmers and skilled craftspeople. They grew **yuca**, sweet potatoes, corn, and other vegetables. They made pottery and baskets to use and trade. The men built dugout canoes both for transportation and for fishing.

The Taíno called the island Borinquen. It means "land of the brave and noble lord."

They Came From Spain

On November 19, 1493, Christopher Columbus landed in Puerto Rico from Spain. At first, the Taíno and other native groups lived peacefully with the Spanish. But in 1508, the Spanish began to colonize the island. The Spanish settlers treated Taínos badly and forced some into slavery. Settlers also brought diseases that sickened many indigenous people. Many Taínos died. Some escaped into the interior of the island.

Puerto Rico is Spanish for "rich port." It was named by explorer Juan Ponce de León.

Juan Ponce de León established the first Spanish settlement on Puerto Rico.

About 1815,
King Ferdinand VII
of Spain began
to encourage his
people to move
to Puerto Rico.
He hoped to collect
money from farming.

King Ferdinand VII of Spain

The new settlers set up large

plantations that raised sugarcane, coffee, and

tobacco. They used the labor of enslaved Africans.

The first major Puerto Rican uprising against

the Spanish took place in 1868. Over the next

decade, Puerto Ricans won some freedoms.

Slavery was outlawed. Life changed again,

however, when Americans arrived on the island.

The Spanish-American War

In 1898, Spain fought against the United States in the Spanish-American War and lost. Puerto Rico and other Spanish colonies were awarded to the United States. At the time, most Puerto Ricans lived in poverty. U.S. companies ran large plantations and kept workers' pay low.

Some people believed that life would get better when they could govern themselves. In 1948, Puerto Rico elected its first governor, Luis Muñoz Marín. Marín helped write Puerto Rico's constitution. He worked to improve education and the economy.

During the Spanish-American War, American troops marched into Puerto Rico in July 1898.

In 1952, Puerto Rico became a **commonwealth** of the United States. This gave the island limited self-rule. Puerto Ricans follow U.S. **federal** laws. They make local laws and elect local government leaders, however. Puerto Ricans are United States citizens, but they don't pay federal taxes or vote in national elections. The island has its own flag and national anthem, but it uses the U.S. dollar and postage stamps.

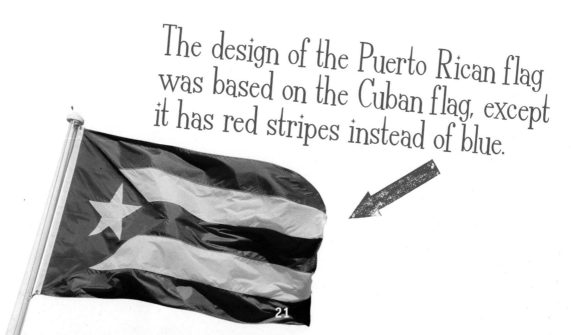

The design of the Puerto Rican flag was based on the Cuban flag, except it has red stripes instead of blue.

For and Against

The political status of Puerto Rico is still under discussion. Some Puerto Ricans would like the territory to become the 51st U.S. state. Some would like full independence. Others are in favor of continuing as a commonwealth. So far, Puerto Ricans have voted three times to remain a commonwealth. By U.S. law, only the U.S. Congress would be able to change that status.

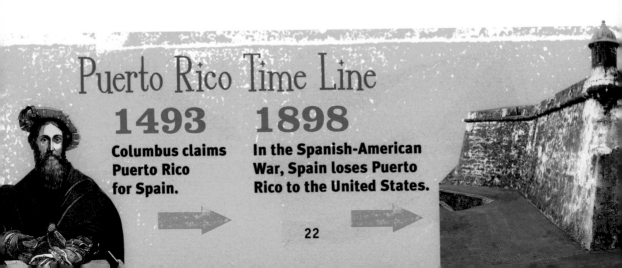

Puerto Rico Time Line

1493
Columbus claims Puerto Rico for Spain.

1898
In the Spanish-American War, Spain loses Puerto Rico to the United States.

There are many reasons why all Puerto Ricans don't agree on independence or statehood. Some believe that statehood would mean losing their **heritage**. They could lose their language, flag, and Olympic team. As a commonwealth, the annual income for workers is among the highest in the Caribbean. Some fear that either statehood or independence would worsen their economy.

1948 ➡ 1952

The people of Puerto Rico elect their first governor, Luis Muñoz Marín. He is known as the father of modern Puerto Rico.

Puerto Rico becomes a U.S. commonwealth.

Many colonial buildings in Old San Juan are painted in bright colors. Shutters on the windows help keep out heat and strong winds.

CHAPTER 4

Arts and Architecture

San Juan is the oldest city in U.S. territory. It was founded in 1521 by Juan Ponce de León.

Much of San Juan is full of modern buildings. High-rise apartments line the shore. But it also has buildings that date from the Spanish colonial days. These buildings are hundreds of years old. They are found in a neighborhood called Old San Juan.

Refinding the Past

In 1955, the Institute of Puerto Rican Culture began to **restore** Old San Juan. More than 400 buildings have been restored. Many are museums. The area also includes two Spanish forts called El Morro and San Cristóbal. El Morro was built to protect Puerto Rico from invaders that came by sea. San Cristóbal was built inland.

Santa Maria Magdalena de Pazzis Cemetery is located just outside the walls of El Morro fort. Many of Puerto Rico's most famous people are buried here.

Oscar Ortiz is an artist who grew up in Puerto Rico. He often uses Puerto Rican themes, such as el jíbaro, in his paintings.

El Jíbaro

In nineteenth-century Puerto Rico, the best farmland was used by European plantation owners. Farmers called *jíbaros* (HEE-bah-rows) kept small farms in the mountains. *El jíbaro* became a symbol of freedom and independence. Many stories feature this character. In art, el jíbaro is often shown wearing a wide-brimmed hat, known as a *pava*. He is usually carrying a machete, a large knife used in farming and for cutting thick vegetation.

Music Matters

The music of Puerto Rico shows the influence of Spanish, African, and Taíno cultures. One Taíno rhythm

Güiros **are rhythm instruments played by scraping notches with a stick.**

instrument is still common today. The Taíno made maracas out of hard-skinned fruits called gourds.

Many styles of music are popular in Puerto Rico. Folk songs in styles called *bomba* and *plena* tell stories to African, Spanish, or Taíno rhythms. A newer style called *reggaeton* mixes Latin American music with reggae, hip hop, and other styles.

Women wear long ruffled skirts for folk dancing. Men usually wear a Panama hat.

28

The most popular dance music to come from Puerto Rico is salsa. A salsa band may include singers, brass instruments, a piano, maracas, conga drums, güiros (GWEE-rohz), and bongos. Salsa dance is fast and energetic to match upbeat salsa rhythms. Marc Anthony is a Puerto Rican American who helped contemporary salsa and other Spanish-language music find new audiences around the world.

Marc Anthony has sold more records than any other salsa singer.

The Big Dish

Imagine a telescope so large, it can be seen from an airplane flying thousands of feet above Earth. The Arecibo (ah-ray-SEE-boh) Observatory is in northwest Puerto Rico. It is the largest single-dish telescope in the world. It began searching space in 1963.

A Giant Radio

The telescope dish is made from about 40,000 aluminum panels. It is 1,000 feet (300 meters) wide. The dish reflects radio signals toward a device that hangs above it. This device sends and receives radio signals to and from deep space.

Amazing Astronomy

The observatory has helped scientists make many discoveries. It helped them locate the first planets outside our solar system. It gathered data used to draw maps of the stars, asteroids, and other objects in the universe.

More than 80,000 people march in the Puerto Rican Day Parade in New York City every June. About two million people watch.

CHAPTER 5

Schooling and Sports

There are almost as many Puerto Ricans living in the United States as there are in Puerto Rico.

It would be hard to separate Puerto Ricans by their ethnic background. Most Puerto Ricans are **descended** in part from the Spanish colonists who started arriving in the 1500s. Many people who were born on the island, however, are a mix. They are descended from native people, such as the Taíno, as well as from Africans and Spanish.

Easier Education

About 100 years ago, only 23 percent of the population in Puerto Rico could read and write. Today that number is nearly 95 percent. The Puerto Rican school system is modeled on the U.S. school system. Puerto Rico controls and funds its own schools, however.

Most children in Puerto Rico wear uniforms to school.

Children in Puerto Rico must attend school between the ages of 5 and 17. At first, the U.S. government required all schools to teach classes in English. However, Puerto Ricans protested and the rule was changed. Since

1949, classes in school are taught in Spanish. However, Puerto Rican students study English for all 12 years that they attend school.

The University of Puerto Rico was founded in 1903. It is the oldest and largest university in Puerto Rico.

Play Ball!

Sports have played a part in the lives of Puerto Ricans for hundreds of years. Taíno people built ball courts and played a game similar to soccer. Soccer is gaining popularity in Puerto Rico today. However, the sport that is most played on the island is baseball.

Many great baseball players come from Puerto Rico. Carlos Delgado has played for the New York Mets and other professional teams.

Carlos Delgado has hit more than 460 home runs!

Puerto Rico has more than 180 teams that are part of the international Little League Baseball network.

There are six teams in the Puerto Rican professional baseball league. Each of these teams is a member of the Caribbean League. They play against other teams from Venezuela, Mexico, and the Dominican Republic. In the United States, the baseball season runs from April until October. But in the Caribbean League, the season lasts from October to March.

On December 28, the town of Hatillo celebrates its annual Mask Festival, called Festival de las Máscaras.

CHAPTER 6

Festivals and Food

Puerto Ricans celebrate different festivals throughout the year. Many towns in Puerto Rico have chosen a **patron saint** from the Roman Catholic Church. Each town celebrates its patron saint's festival, called *fiesta patronal*. The celebrations include dances, parades, and special foods.

The Hatillo Mask Festival has been celebrated ever since the town was founded in 1823.

Island Spices

Like the music, Puerto Rican food is a blend of Taíno, Spanish, and African flavors. Soups, stews, and rice are popular dishes. Some of these are spiced with lime juice, cloves, and cinnamon. Many recipes include a kind of sauce called *sofrito*. This is made from onions, garlic, cilantro, tomatoes, and green and red peppers.

Stands along the beach commonly sell cod fish fritters and *pastelillos,* or fried turnovers filled with meat and spices.

The Plantain Migration

One fruit, called a plantain, traveled a long way to reach Puerto Rico. When enslaved Africans were brought to work on plantations, they brought it with them.

An African dish called *mofongo* is made from mashed plantains mixed with garlic and meat. Plantains are also eaten fried, stuffed, or grilled. Boiled plantains make a hot breakfast. Candied plantains are a sweet treat.

Fresh and fried plantains

Looking to the Future

Puerto Rico's traditions have stayed strong through centuries of political shifts. That shows no signs of changing. In 2008, the New Progressive Party came to power. Party members hope to make Puerto Rico the 51st state. Only time will tell whether Puerto Rico will find success as a U.S. state, independent nation, or something in-between. ★

The Puerto Rico Convention Center in San Juan was opened in 2005. It is the largest convention center in the Caribbean and one of the most modern in all of Latin America.

Official name: Commonwealth of Puerto Rico

Area including islands and inland water:
3,515 sq. mi. (9,103 sq. km)

Major Cities: San Juan, Bayamón, Ponce, Carolina

Number of islands: 4 major islands; several tiny islands

Population: About 4 million

Religions: 85 percent Roman Catholic, 15 percent Protestant, and others

Currency: U.S. dollar

Number of television stations: 32

Highest point above sea level: Cerro de Punta 4,389 ft. (1,338 m)

Did you find the truth?

(T) Tiny frogs can rain from trees in Puerto Rico.

(F) Puerto Rico consists of two islands.

Resources

Books

Bjorklund, Ruth. *Puerto Rico* (It's My State!). Tarrytown, NY: Marshall Cavendish/ Benchmark, 2007.

Burgan, Michael. *Puerto Rico* (From Sea to Shining Sea). New York: Children's Press, 2003.

Feeney, Kathy. *Puerto Rico*: *Facts and Symbols*. Mankato, MN: Hilltop Books, 2001.

Foster, Leila Merrell. *A Visit to Puerto Rico*. Chicago: Heinemann Library, 2008.

Hernandez, Romel. *Puerto Rico* (Discovering the Caribbean). Philadelphia: Mason Crest Publishers, 2004.

Levy, Patricia, and Nazry Bahrawi. *Puerto Rico* (Cultures of the World). Tarrytown, NY: Marshall Cavendish/Benchmark, 2005.

Stille, Darlene R. *Puerto Rico* (America the Beautiful). New York: Children's Press, 2009.

Organizations and Web Sites

Boricua Kids

www.elboricua.com/BoricuaKids.html
Read up on Puerto Rican food, learn folk songs, and do some coloring.

CIA - The World Factbook: Puerto Rico

www.cia.gov/library/publications/the-world-factbook/geos/rq.html
Get to know facts and figures about the Puerto Rican people, government, and economy.

Puerto Rico and the American Dream

www.prdream.com/about.html
View the online film galleries and find time lines of the history, culture, and politics of Puerto Rico.

Places to Visit

Clemente Soto Vélez Cultural and Educational Centre Inc.

107 Suffolk Street
New York, NY 10002
(212) 260 4080
http://csvcenter.com/2005/
Find out all about Puerto Rican and Latino culture.

Institute of Puerto Rican Arts and Culture

3015 West Division Street
Chicago, IL 60622
(773) 486 8345
www.iprac.org/home.htm
Take part in arts and culture programs and see exhibitions year-round.

Important Words

archipelago (ar-kuh-PEL-uh-goh) – a group of small islands

commercial crop – crops grown to be sold for a profit

commonwealth – a place, or territory, that is partially governed by the people who live there

coral – a substance found underwater, made up of the skeletons of tiny sea creatures

descend (di-SEND) – to belong to a later generation of the same family

federal – relating to the central government of a group of states or territories

heritage – valued traditions handed down from generation to generation

imported – referring to goods that are brought into a country from another country

indigenous (in-DIJ-uh-nuhss) – describing the original people living in an area

patron saint – a saint that is believed to look after a particular country or group

plantation – a large farm where crops are grown to sell; workers often live on part of the land

restore – to bring back to a former or normal condition

yuca – the root of a tropical tree that can be eaten

Index

Page numbers in **bold** indicate illustrations

About the Author

Howard Gutner has a degree in journalism from the University of Illinois and has written books about the *Titanic* and the Great Chicago Fire, as well as historical fiction. He also loves writing about the countries he has visited. He visited Puerto Rico on a cruise of the Caribbean Sea in 2004. He makes his home in Brooklyn, New York.